BULLET
JOURNALING

TRACK YOUR PAST, HACK YOUR
PRESENT, AND DREAM YOUR FUTURE!

EARNEST CINNAMON

TABLE OF CONTENTS

INTRODUCTION

Keep a journal. How many times have you read or heard about this advice on self-care and productivity?

By now, you already have ideas as to why you should heed to the said advice. You might have tried it before, but felt like it didn't work. Perhaps journaling isn't right for you. Why not try something that's more flexible and more likely to suit your needs?

Introducing bullet journaling. This book contains proven tips on how to get started and how to remain inspired on your foray into the latest productivity craze.

With the help of this book, you'll understand what makes bullet journaling different from the use of a diary, journal, or planner. Get to know the basics of the original method as well.

Contrary to those snaps of fancy bullet journal spreads, you don't need plenty of materials to get started. You just need a notebook and a pen at first. If you like to add some spice and unleash your artistic side, this book will give you suggestions on what kind of materials you should look for and how you can use them.

The main highlights of this book are the guides on how you should plan and create your bullet journal, fondly called as bujo. How do you make yours unique and functional? Where will you get inspiration when you're low on creative juices? Most importantly, how can you use it to track your past, hack your present, and dream your future? This book will answer those questions and more.

Right after the last chapter of this book, you'll come across the 15-Day Bullet Journaling Challenge. This will inspire and walk you through the initial steps of your upcoming creative and productive pursuit.

Thanks for downloading this book, I hope you enjoy it!

WHAT IS BULLET JOURNALING?

Pinterest and Instagram are filled with snaps of artful bujo covers and pages. At first glance, it seems like bullet journaling is a way of showcasing one's creativity. However, not a lot of people are aware that there's actually an original method, and it's not as elaborate as you might have expected.

Ryder Carroll, the designer of bullet journaling, envisioned his brainchild to be a system that will help people become more organized. He also tried to use it to address the difficulty of coming up with sentences like that in simple journaling.

THE IDEA OF RAPID LOGGING

Writing by hand helps you remember things much better than recording info in your phone or computer. However, not everyone is keen on spending minutes jotting down sentences detailing what happened during the day or what to do tomorrow. As a solution, Carroll introduced the idea of rapid logging.

Basically, rapid logging is the way you're supposed to write on a bujo. It's referred to as bullet journaling's language for that reason. It simply entails writing a keyword or phrase.

THE BULLET

In terms of bullet journaling, bullet is deemed as the format of an entry. It's made up of a keyword or phrase preceded by an indicator or two.

THE TRIO OF BASIC ENTRIES

Tasks, events, and notes are the three basic entries you'll record on your bujo. These are far from being groundbreaking. What makes the bullet journaling method special, though, is that it encourages you to keep various reminders in one notebook.

Obviously, tasks are the things you typically write on your to-do list. In bullet journaling, these tasks are categorized into five: complete, incomplete, migrated, scheduled, and irrelevant.

Events are made up of past and future happenings. You're supposed to write these down concisely and objectively. Don't forget to add the dates.

As for notes, these can be a lot of things. These can be ideas, learnings, or realizations. These can even include inspirational messages.

SYMBOLS AND SIGNIFIERS

Putting your to-do lists, shopping list, and all other reminders in one place seems like a recipe for disaster. The original method has a solution for that though.

You can count on symbols to indicate the nature of each bujo entry. The standard bullet sign is used for tasks, small circle for events, and dash for notes. You can also use signifiers to add more context in an entry. For example, you can add an asterisk before the symbol sign to entail that a task is a priority.

COLLECTIONS

Aside from symbols and signifiers, the concept of collections makes bujos organized. A collection is about entries that are similar or related in a way. It usually fills a page or spread. The four basic collections are index, daily log, monthly log, and future log.

These are the core features of the original bullet journaling method. You can choose to stick to this or you can customize the method to fit your own needs.

CHAPTER 1:

How to be in Charge of
Your Journaling

Journaling is an age-old practice across different cultures. Its purpose spans from improving your writing, preserving your memories, keeping reminders, and having an outlet to express and process emotions in a healthy way. Another great thing about this practice is that you have full control on how to do it.

But are you really in charge of your journaling? Mass media and social media platforms abound with descriptions on how it should look like. The ideal way is done before bedtime and on a study table. The journal writer starts off by jotting down the date on the upper right corner of the first blank page.

Some proceed by making a salutation, with Dear Diary as the most popular option. Some personalize their diary or journal by giving them nicknames and addressing them in such in the salutation, body, and closing of the entry. Others go straight to the body right after writing the date.

The bulk of a journal entry is all about experiences and realizations. The passages are featured in cursive handwriting that's uniform, legible, and elegant-looking. Moreover, the written entry is free from grammatical errors, misspellings, and handwriting mistakes.

THE REALISTIC WAY

With such depictions of journaling, it's easy to understand why some people get intimidated by the practice. If you're one of them, you should know that journaling is far from being error-free. Furthermore, even avid journal writers deviate from the supposed norms of the practice. These shouldn't come as a surprise since everyone has his or her own preferences of doing things.

First of all, not everyone likes to write on a study table, let alone have it in the bedroom. Some do their planning, alongside writing, on a dining table. Others do it on countertops. With a hardbound journal, you can even write while sitting on your bed. Or with a lightweight and small notebook, you can do journaling while on a train ride.

As for the time you should do it, there are varying anecdotes on what works and what doesn't. It's no secret that some people prefer to do their writing while sipping their morning coffee. Some do it during lunch breaks, class hours, or even work hours. The recommended minutes that you should do it may span from five minutes to half an hour.

The usual advice is to write once a day on a daily basis. However, it's normal for even long-time journal writers to skip on some days due to sickness, tiredness, or lack of motivation.

Content-wise, you can expect it to be about personal thoughts. Some try to focus on details and their emotions. Others put stress on their reflections. There are also those who can strike balance on the said aspects. However, it took them years of practicing writing and meditation to have such kind of ability. If you don't have much experience writing, it may be hard for you to come up with something that can be considered journal-worthy.

Another challenging part of regular journaling is the act of writing by hand. Not everyone has great handwriting. Aside from that, you should expect misspellings, omissions, cross-outs, and additional notes on the edges of a regular journal.

The realistic way of journaling is best described as ever evolving. It's a process full of trial and error. It's learning what works for you and sticking to it. In case you outgrow your own method, you're free from modifying it or even take a break from journaling.

As many journaling enthusiasts point out, the journal is an extension of oneself. From its cover to its pages, you're not just recording your thoughts or expressing yourself. You're also showing your personality and aspirations in it. If you make mistakes or take a break, it only means you're imperfect, like all other humans.

HOW TO BE IN CHARGE

Journaling in your own way is a manifestation of being in charge of the practice. Aside from that, you can also exercise your full control by setting a time to start it and committing to it.

One of the usual mistakes of beginners is that they wait for a significant event in their life to begin their journaling journey. If you do this, it means you're letting a certain date or a milestone dictate when you're going to start. You shouldn't wait for long. If you do, you're allowing yourself to entertain thoughts on how challenging journaling could be. You may notice this when you think of starting but you end up making excuses on why you shouldn't start yet.

When it comes to the writing process, you can kick off with a single paragraph. You can write about how excited you are for your foray into journaling. You can also take notes on why you're about to start it.

In terms of formatting, committing to a single paragraph per journaling session may help you stick to the practice right away. Filling a full page or two for the first time may come across as mentally draining.

The best time to write is before or after your peak times. Peak times refer to those hours that you're in your optimal condition to work.

While it will be beneficial if you do your journaling during these hours, you may feel drained to do the more pertinent tasks in your non-peak hours.

CONTENT VARIETY

In addition to experiences during the day, it's normal for journal writers to include reminders about tasks and events in the passages or on the margins of their journal pages. While writing by hand is proven to be better in helping you memorize things, your reminders may get lost in blocks of paragraphs or look like clutter in your journal.

For those who want to do more and be better, it's more advisable to use a planner instead of a journal. But if you're like most people, you'll prefer something that gives you a space for your thoughts, along with your tasks and other reminders.

That's what a bujo is for. In the original bullet journaling method, you'll need to write an index which works like the table of contents for the journal. Herein, you gather all the titles of your collections and arrange them according to their page numbers. Aside from titles and their page numbers, this also features the list of symbols, signifiers and their respective meanings. The index usually comes after the title page of a bujo. It's basically the first collection.

The second recommended collection is the future log. In this collection, you list down the relevant events and tasks for a specific month, week or day. It often comes with a calendar of the whole year. It can span from one spread up to three consecutive spreads. This can highlight your year goals as well.

The next one is the monthly log or simply referred as monthly. For this collection, you can further break down tasks for an event or a goal. You also include your regular monthly or quarterly tasks herein. Think of grocery shopping, home maintenance, health checkups, and hair trimmings. The monthly may simply feature the name of the month or it may come with a calendar of the said month.

The daily log or daily is meant for days filled with numerous tasks and events to remember. The date and list of reminders are the basic components of a daily. In some bujos, the specific time for certain reminders are also indicated. A daily may also include a section for the day's highlights. This is kind of similar to standard journaling. However, the highlights put more emphasis on the defining moments and tend to eliminate mundane details. Additionally, instead of sentences or paragraphs, the highlights are written using only keywords.

In case there's a task or event that takes up an entire week or two, a weekly log or weekly may be better than a daily log. A weekly isn't included in the four core types of collections. But if you look online, you'll find plenty of bullet journaling enthusiasts who prefer weeklies than dailies. There are even those who accommodate these two in their respective bujos.

If there are days when you don't have much to do, it may be better to make a daily instead of a weekly. A weekly may not look well because there'll be days that won't get filled. Nevertheless, if you think you'll write about the highlights on non-busy days, either a daily or weekly may suit your needs.

These aren't the only kinds of collections that can go in your bujo. All those creative trackers and lists on your social media feeds are actually forms of collections.

A title is the basic element of a collection. For the four core collections, you can use their basic names as titles. You can also personalize the titles if you want. As for the entries for each collection, they could be song titles, movie titles, book titles, character names, quotes, pictures, sketches, stickers, swatches, or a combination of those.

Reading list, music playlist, and movie recommendations are three of the popular kinds of optional collections. They are typically written in a list form. Those who are artistic and daring try to compile their reading list in sketches of books in a shelf. For music playlists, some sketch a screen capture of a digital playlist. When it comes to movie recommendations, some bullet journaling enthusiasts draw a film reel and list the movie titles therein.

Swatches are also among the well-loved collections. Featuring samples of a set of pens is one of the most popular swatches. You can write the name and/or number of the pen on the side of its sample.

A collection of washi tape strips is an essential in many bujos as well. Washi tapes come in various designs. You can find plenty of florals, patterns, and even cartoon characters. Some washi tapes can be costly but the majority tends to be inexpensive. Additionally, these supplies can serve many purposes in bullet journaling. Aside from creating a swatch as a collection, you can use it to decorate your bujo or to mask mistakes inside.

In the succeeding chapters of this book, you'll find more types of collections. These could fit your planning needs for your meals, health, business, finances, and more. For the meantime, head on to the next chapter to discover some possible sources of inspiration to make your bujo as unique as you.

CHAPTER 2:

Inspirations to Make Your
Bullet Journal Unique

Bullet journals are innately unique. After all, you can copy designs and handwriting but it's not like you'll mimic the logs of someone else. However, there's a part of you that wish you can create a unique and functional bujo.

Instead of drawing inspiration from photos of bujo spreads online, think about yourself: who you are, what you are, and what you aspire to be. Develop your ideas from there. Below are possible sources of inspiration that will surely make your bujo one of a kind.

YOUR ACTUAL SELF

What's a better source of inspiration than your actual self? You can glue a picture of yourself on the cover or title page of your bujo. If you have enough confidence in your drawing skills, why not make your own portrait instead? Aside from your self-image, you can also derive inspiration from your family, work, or the organizations and institutions you're affiliated with. On the inner cover of your bujo, write down your name or create your own version of "This book belongs to" section.

You can also create a profile of yourself on the cover, inside cover, or title page of your bujo. In addition to a picture, you can add your name, nickname, birthday, address, and company. Or, you can also put less pertinent information such as birthstone or zodiac sign.

YOUR DREAMS

Picture the ideal version of yourself or your life. Draw them or representations in your bujo. You can also write key phrases or print images and glue them. You may even try making collages or diagrams featuring your life goals.

MEMORABLE LOCATIONS AND DREAM DESTINATIONS

Through bullet journaling, celebrate where you came from, where you've been and/or where you're living right now. Decorate the covers and pages with symbols representing those places. You can create collections based on the popular people, landmarks, and establishments in your area. For these collections, you can add pictures of the people and/or the places mentioned or featured.

Don't forget about your dream destinations. Do you wish to visit a certain place within the year? Make it a prominent aspect of your bujo by attaching a photograph, sketch, or printed name of the place right on the cover.

It's also okay if you want to keep your bujo as simple as possible. You can make it unique through your handwriting and signifiers. For your signifiers, you can use a certain pen color instead of symbols or letters.

While useful, it's not enough to simply have inspirations for your bujo's design and content. To help you sustain your interest in the practice, learn, remember, and earn many of the benefits of bullet journaling.

CHAPTER 3:

Benefits of Finally Upgrading to a Bullet Journal

For some people, phone and computer applications are enough to record pertinent information and set reminders. Others rely on sticky notes, memo pads, and even boards. There are also those who stick to the good old planners. For the affluent ones, they can always hire a secretary or an assistant to do the record-keeping.

Each of the said solutions, however, comes with one or more disadvantages. Your device may malfunction and thus, you lose access to your reminders and records. Sticky notes and memo pads may fly away or get mixed up with clutter.

Entries on boards may get erased. Boards aren't that portable as well. You might also not want to keep a stock of chalks and washable pens. Don't forget about the task of cleaning the board.

Planners are preformatted and thus, have pre-determined spaces for your daily logs. What if you have more tasks to write about? In some days, you may have fewer things to do, leaving your planner with some wasted spaces.

Moreover, you might not be able to reuse an unused planner in the next years because of the pre-printed dates in them. Many planners even have the year featured on the cover. You can hide these things but admit it: it's not that inspiring to write when your planner has plenty of coverups for some parts.

As for hiring a secretary or assistant, not everyone has the capacity and the need for such. Additionally, there's no guarantee that the hired person won't make mistakes or won't resign at one point.

To be fair, bullet journaling isn't perfect either. However, it tends to be more effective for many people who have different needs. Below are the top benefits of upgrading from the use of planners, sticky notes, and other tools to the use of a bujo.

SERVING MULTIPLE FUNCTIONS

A bujo is like a regular journal, planner, notepad, tracker, calendar, sketchpad, calligraphy pad, and scrapbook rolled into one. Like a typical journal and scrapbook, it helps you preserve memories. It also enables you to take notes and to make your to-do lists, similar to that of a notepad and calendar.

If you want to unleash your creative side, you can use a page or a spread to sketch or do calligraphy. Depending on the paper's quality, you may even paint pages using watercolor. You can also feature a collage. If you're adept at making designs by paper cutting, you may likewise apply it on the edges of your bujo's pages.

With all the different kinds of lists you can include in your bujo, it's safe to say that it can help you in many aspects of your life. It's beneficial for your entertainment needs because when you're bored, you can refer to the book or movie recommendations that you've written in your bujo. Having trackers in your bujo may also help you develop habits.

SPEEDING UP RECORD-KEEPING AND PROCESSING

Rapid logging—bullet journaling's very language—won't be called as such for no reason. As its name entails, you'll record entries in your bujo in a quick manner. You don't have to worry about grammar because you're just going to jot down phrases. Thanks to simple symbols and signifiers, you only need a few strokes to indicate the status and priority level of a task.

MINIMIZING STRESSORS

Having different kinds of mediums for your reminders is going to stress you out instead of helping you focus on tasks. With a single notebook for all your needs, you'll feel more at ease knowing you don't have to think hard when you're unsure where a certain reminder is.

Additionally, when there are thoughts that are bothering you, you can use your bujo like a typical journal and write down those thoughts. If you don't like the idea of writing, you can simply create a mind map. Instead of paragraphs, sum up those distracting thoughts in words and connect them with related topics accordingly.

The act of designing can also serve as a way for you to unwind. Aside from designing though, you can record your worries and make a list of possible solutions in your bujo.

IMPROVING MINDFULNESS

Both journaling and bullet journaling could help you become more mindful. With the typical journaling, however, you'll tend to pay more attention to details and your emotions. In contrast, bullet journaling trains you to focus more on goals and what you've accomplished so far.

ENHANCING RESOURCEFULNESS

The way you personalize your bujo will surely inspire you to become more creative. If you're eager to start without feeling the need to buy supplies, you can recycle an old notebook or create your own journal. Aside from that, you can also experiment with the many types of decors you can use.

INSTILLING THANKFULNESS

Many bullet journaling enthusiasts have a page exclusive for their gratitude list. With this kind of collection, you're more likely to pay attention to good things that happen to you in a day or week instead of focusing on the bad ones.

DOING MORE

Bullet journaling may have different meanings for each enthusiast. However, no one can deny that its ultimate benefit has a lot to do with productivity. With the reminders on your tasks, you'll be able to remember them more and thus, do more. You may find satisfaction by designing, but it's through knowing your priorities and completing your important tasks that you'll feel more fulfilled.

Through bullet journaling, you may even discover new skills and hobbies to try. But first, you have to make it a habit. In this case, the next chapter will help you with various tips and tricks.

CHAPTER 4:

Tips and Tricks

––––––––––––––––––––––––––––––––––––––

Bullet journaling isn't that hard to do. Nonetheless, knowing and applying some tips and tricks will make the activity less intimidating and help you retain interest in it. Below are many of the tips and tricks you need to know.

ON BUYING A BUJO

1. If you intend to buy a bujo, look for a dotted one. This tends to be more beginner-friendly compared to blank or grid journals. As for the ruled one, it tends to be the least flexible.

2. Find out if a bujo is fountain pen or watercolor-friendly in case you like to use the said materials for writing and designing.

3. Bujo-wise, never mistake a page as a sheet. One sheet actually entails four consecutive pages.

4. If you're unsure about the right journal size for your needs, you can stick to either an A5 or A6 journal.

5. In case you like to go eco-friendly, you can buy a journal made from recycled paper.

6. Don't buy a custom-made bujo since it's your first time.

7. If you want your bujo to retain its shape, choose a journal that has thick cover and a closing. A closing can simply be a rubber band, garter, or thread that comes along with some notebooks.

ON CHOOSING A PEN AND OTHER WRITING MATERIALS

1. Try using a ballpoint pen, gel pen, and fountain pen and find out what suits your handwriting needs.

2. When shopping for a brand of pens for the first time, just buy one, two, or the pack with the least number of pens.

3. Invest on a white ink pen. It can work as a correction pen or a color pen.

4. Know that color pencils are not entirely the same. Nowadays, some color pencils are actually meant to be used as watercolor or calligraphy pencils.

5. Instead of getting calligraphy pens, go for washable brush pens. You can choose either soft tip or hard tip.

6. Always buy your pens from a store instead of individual sellers online.

ON DESIGNING

1. Always use a pencil when sketching or making outlines.

2. Use a template for doing circles and other shapes.

3. If you like drawing characters, you can download guides or print characters and trace them using a pantograph.

4. Stock up on paper stencils or make your own.

ON USING WATERCOLOR

1. Cover pages you don't want to get watercolor stains on using a plastic cover or at least two sheets of scrap paper.

2. You can also use washi tape to cover some parts of the page and apply watercolor on the exposed parts.

3. Don't use too much water because it will leave behind water stains.

ON LETTERING

1. Apply the basic faux calligraphy rule: thick for downstroke, thin for upstroke.

2. Combine a fancy font with a simple one. If the words in the first line are written using the fancy font, use the simple font for the words in the second. Do it alternately.

3. Another option is to write words in the first line in bold and capital letters, while the words in the second line are in small and thin fonts.

ON MARKING

1. Mark the edge of your bujo with washi tape. One color or style of the washi tape may indicate related collections.

2. You can reuse an old bookmark or buy a new one as a way to mark the last page you've filled in your journal or to indicate a weekly or daily.

3. You can also apply threading. In bullet journaling, threading refers to the act of putting a page number beside another page number to indicate related contents.

ON FINDING SUPPORT AND GETTING TIPS

1. Join online groups and forums dedicated to bullet journaling.
2. Participate in bullet journaling challenges online or initiate one yourself.
3. Attend fairs meant for those who love art supplies.
4. Collaborate with other Pinterest users who are also into bullet journaling. You can contribute into bujo-related boards.

ON MAKING MISTAKES

1. Cover them with a sticker, washi tape, or picture.
2. You can use either a correction pen or a correction tape.
3. If you missed to fill some trackers on some days, make a new signifier indicating that you forgot to fill them.
4. Poke fun at your mistake. For example, if you wrote January on the title page of your February monthly, you can write the phrase comes before February right under the mistake.

ON JOURNALING

1. Go over your daily after you wake up and before you sleep.
2. Don't stress yourself over tasks that you've realized are irrelevant or collections that you've failed to complete.
3. Just enjoy keeping yourself productive and organized with the help of bullet journaling.

CHAPTER 5:

Past Log

With a bujo, you can discard various papers and notebooks containing important records and reminders. You just have to keep original copies of signed documents such as house purchase, lease agreement, and receipts. But before you shred and throw out the irrelevant papers and notebooks, make sure you transfer the pertinent info into your bujo. These will comprise your past log.

A past log isn't among the most popular logs out there. However, it can be beneficial in helping you reduce the number of records you have to keep. The process of creating this log also encourages you to sort out important and irrelevant reminders. It will help you retain memories from your pre-bullet journaling years. Your past log can be made up of just one or many of the collections below.

MILESTONES

You may be a first-timer in bullet journaling, but you certainly are not in other aspects of your life. Celebrate all your first-times and other accomplishments in a collection about your milestones. You can either mix or separate milestones in your personal and professional lives.

TRAVELS

For the wanderlust, a collection based on one's travels is a must-have. You can arrange your list based on the dates or based on the locations. For example, you may separate local travels from international ones. For international travels, indicate the airlines and your review of their service.

Include memorabilia such as photos, tickets, and stamps. Add captions as well. If there are memorable encounters, express them into key phrases beside the memorabilia and caption.

BONDING TIMES

Thanks to social networking sites and mobile phones, it's easier to message and update your loved ones nowadays. However, ask yourself when was the last time you've spent moments with your significant other, family, and friends without the screens and filters. If you're the type who value relationships, you can make a collection based on previous bonding moments with your loved ones.

As for plans for your next bonding times, include them in either your monthly or yearly. To prepare for this, it will be ideal to feature a list of your loved ones' contact info. These may cover phone numbers and social media accounts.

SERVICES, SUBSCRIPTIONS, PURCHASES, WARRANTIES, AND INVESTMENTS

It's advisable that you keep your receipts and service agreements for services such as HVAC inspection, roofing repair, and car maintenance. Aside from these, it's also recommended that you record the dates when the services were rendered. Based on the receipts and service agreement, indicate the key service, date, and service provider when you feature them as entries to a collection.

Make a separate page for warranty periods as well. This could cover warranties from services and major purchases. Indicate the maker or service provider, along with their contact info, in this page.

Major purchases refer to appliances, furniture sets, power tools, gadgets, and other expensive equipment that you buy for yourself. However, the most notable purchases are properties and vehicles. Make sure you dedicate a page or two in your past log detailing the major purchase, when and where you bought them, and how much they cost. Aside from services and purchases, include subscriptions as well.

Investments are also worth including in your past log. Major purchases may be considered are investments if you think you're likely to sell them in the future. But as much as possible, you should only include your home and car in the investment section in your past log. Financial investments on partnerships or company stocks are more suitable for the section.

LOANS

It's scary to think about student loans, car loans, and mortgages. However, it's even scarier when you miss a payment and risk your financial stability for penalties.

To help avoid missing payments and to help ensure you have enough money to pay for your debts, include your loans in your past log. You can opt to get debt consolidation service if you have various loans. By getting such service, you'll just focus on a single repayment per month or per quarter. Additionally, it's easier to create a log for your loans if you're only paying for one. Nonetheless, you're free to make a separate log for each loan.

When including your loans in your past log, write the name of the lender, the original amount of the loan, the interest rate, and how much you've paid so far. For upcoming repayments, you can include it in a yearly, monthly, or weekly.

Before you create your past log, it's ideal to have the index page and future log first. The past log may come next to the future log. By doing this, you can go over your past log and make additional entries in your future log about events and tasks you should remember.

CHAPTER 6:

Present Log

If you dwell too much on your past, you may end up regretting many things. If you look forward excessively, you may miss existing opportunities and lose touch of the present. You should simply look back and look forward when you need a guide with how to live your present life.

Aside from that, you can also engage in bullet journaling to exercise and enhance mindfulness. Being mindful helps you live in the moment. Below are some types of collection that you may form part of your present log.

DAILY AND WEEKLY

You've already learned about daily and weekly in previous chapters. These are meant to be forms of present log.

If your tasks and events go beyond 15, it will be better to categorize them instead of just recording them as a list in your daily or in one day in your weekly. Group them into categories such as home and family, school, work, and miscellaneous. You can likewise opt to arrange them based on which task you should do first. Indicate the time and duration for each task as well.

HIGHLIGHTS OF THE DAY

As its name suggest, this collection is about the moments that stood out the most during the day. You can opt to include it in a daily or create a separate collection for this. Keep it short and simple by writing key phrases, but you can add some expressions to show what you've felt about those moments.

NOTE/S TO SELF

Do your own cheerleading instead of waiting for others to do it for you. You can do this by writing mini pep talks to yourself beside or before your daily.

RANDOM MIND DUMP

Pour your heart out in a mind dump section in your bujo. This helps free yourself from the possibility of overthinking about certain things. No matter how crazy your thoughts seem to be, write this down so you can do a better assessment.

Meal plans and trackers also belong to the present log portion of a bujo. Learn more about the different kinds of collections in the last four chapters of this book. For the meantime, dream your future with the help of the succeeding chapter.

CHAPTER 7:

Future Log

―――――――――――――――――――――

The future is full of uncertainties. However, you can navigate through it with the help of good planning and preparation. There are many ways you can plan for your future. One of which is through bullet journaling. In your bujo, you can make yearly goals and bucket lists as part of your future log or as separate collections.

THE YEAR IN A GLANCE

Some bullet journaling enthusiasts refer to their future logs or yearly as the year in a glance. After all, you get to see the entire calendar for the year, as well as check relevant events and tasks, in just a few pages.

The yearly helps you stay on track all throughout the year. It also provides you bases when you make assessments of yourself and the things you've done. When you lack ideas for upcoming daily or weekly, you can refer to your future log for things you have yet to accomplish.

BUCKET LIST

Make sure cross out many of your bucket list entries by featuring it as a collection right after your yearly log. Your bucket list can be as fewer than 10 or up to 100. You can group them together based on their similarities. For example, skydiving and mountain climbing can go under the extreme sports category. The places you want to visit, the foods you want to eat, the people you want to meet, and other things you want to experience belong to this section.

By including your bucket list in your bujo, you help create a savings tracker for the money needed to accomplish some entries. You can also make a collection based on the documents and other things you have to prepare for some activities.

CHAPTER 8:

Making
Your Own Journal

If you think a collection is inappropriate for a bujo, you should know that some enthusiasts even make trackers for sex, swearing, and other seemingly unsuitable topics. As long as it's not unethical and illegal, you shouldn't hold back making your own journal about yourself and your needs.

MINIMALIST, ARTISTIC, OR MIXED

When it comes to bullet journaling, you can stick to being minimalistic or artistic. You can also opt to mix elements of minimalism and art in your bujo. If you're a perfectionist, the minimalist way may fit your personality and lifestyle better. If you're the spontaneous type, you can design your bujo in whatever way you want.

FAVORITES AND INTERESTS

Featuring your favorites in your bujo is one of the quickest ways to fall in love with bullet journaling. Make a sketch, add a picture, or create a profile of your favorite celebrity. Decorate the pages with washi tapes that has logos related to your go-to movie. Write the lyrics of your comfort song on the cover or on one of your bujo pages. There are countless of ways you can incorporate your loves in bullet journaling.

Don't restrict your favorites to celebrities, movies, TV shows, books, songs, games, and fictional characters. You can even try to design your bujo based on your go-to memes, websites, apps, catchphrases, and other pop culture references.

If you're not into pop culture, you can focus on the mundane like your favorite color, food, or hangout place. You can likewise find inspirations in your hobbies.

If you're a foodie, a gardener, an avid DIY-er, or a space enthusiast, there are plenty of stickers that you can use to decorate your bujo. You can even make bujo collections based on your hobby.

For instance, if you're a foodie, you can create a list of food you want to try before you die. You can draw your favorite dishes and desserts. You can even make a collection based on your favorite recipes or recipes you want to try.

In case you love gardening, you can compile cultivation tips in a page or two. You can also create a tracker for seeds you planted. You can incorporate your love for plants when decorating your bujo pages or trackers as well. Another option is to use plant- or gardening-related symbols as your signifiers.

CHAPTER 9:

Making
Your Meal Planning

Healthy eating is a habit that billions of people still can't do. For some, it could be due to their finances. But if you're among those who have poor eating habits because you're too lazy or uninspired to make changes, creating collections for your meals may help a lot.

WEEKLY MEAL PLAN

To make a weekly meal plan, start by listing down dishes and even drinks. You can do this by yourself if you're living alone or cooking meals for yourself. But if you're living with your family or if you have roommates whom you share meals with, you need to ask them what they want to eat for the upcoming week. Don't forget to account the ingredients they can't eat and the dishes they don't like.

The next step is to write down recipes. If you run out of ideas, you can always search online and add your own twists.

For your weekly meal plan, make sure you write down the specific food and drinks for breakfast, lunch, and dinner of each day of the week. You should also make a section for the snacks.

Make sure you put the amount of servings as well. This will help you plan cooking dishes by batch. This means you can save time and effort for cooking as you simply have to re-heat what you have prepared beforehand.

RECIPES

In the recipe sections of your bujo, be as detailed as possible. Enumerate all the ingredients—including the condiments—that you need to use for each recipe. You should also mention the measurements. Don't forget the amount of servings each recipe can produce. If you can, decorate the recipe sections with the sketches of the ingredients and cooking tools. You may also include a picture of the list.

CHAPTER 10:

Keep Your Bullet Journal

Mental health isn't the only aspect of wellness that benefits from bullet journaling. Even your physical and emotional health can enjoy advantages as well. After all, bullet journaling enables you to develop and track healthy habits. Aside from healthy eating, it can also help you when it comes to getting quality sleep, finding out if a workout routine is helping you lose weight, and many more.

SLEEP LOG

The sleep log is among the most popular bujo collections out there. This is actually a good thing since a lot of people are dealing with productivity and health issues due to poor sleeping habits.

Aside from making a sleep log, some opt to create a separate nap log. You can also do so but if you want to save time, just feature them in a single collection. Indicate the number of hours for your sleep or nap, along with the specific time of the day. As much as possible, mark your sleep log right after you wake up.

MOOD TRACKER

A mood tracker usually comes next after sleep log. It's up to you how to categorize your mood. Your categories can be as simple as happy, sad, mad, anxious, or mixed up.

WORKOUT CALENDAR

For the busy bee in you, spending an hour a day to work out may be too much to do, most especially if you're not aiming for a bodybuilder's physique. If you just want to keep your body in a healthy condition, you can choose basic workouts for each body part. Afterwards, schedule each or a group of basic exercises for a 10- to 15-minute workout session per day.

MILE TRACKER

Whether you're gearing up for a marathon or just wanting to reap the benefits of walking and/or running, a mile tracker in your bujo will suit you. An app that tracks the number of your footsteps and the miles you've covered will be helpful for creating this collection. In your mile tracker, indicate how far you've walked or run in a certain day. You can write a target for this collection. It's also helpful to feature what you want as reward once you've hit your target.

WATER INTAKE LOG

Who tracks their water intake? Apparently, many bujo enthusiasts do so because they tend to work, play, watch, or rest without taking a sip of water. If you're one of those who tend to consume more coffee, tea, sweetened drinks, soft drinks, or alcohol, this type of fitness log can be beneficial.

The water intake log doesn't have to be complex. It can simply cover a quarter or half of a page. It should have a section for the amount of water you've drunk (in liters). It should also have a portion that indicates the day. If you drink non-water beverages, you may opt to indicate so using a different color than that of the pen you're using to mark your water intake.

WEIGHT TRACKER

Whether you're trying to lose, gain, or maintain your current weight, the weight tracker is a must-have in your bujo. This fitness tracker should occupy at least a page. On the top of the page, it should have your main goal regarding your weight. You need to provide a weight range as well. Don't write a specific weight because it will be stressful for you if you restrict yourself to that.

In addition to the weight tracker, it will be helpful if you write down benefits of the loss, gain, or maintenance of your weight. Based on your weight goal, you can also mention tips and tricks to achieve it, in a section beside or along with your tracker.

SKIN CARE ROUTINE

For this log, feature the perks you want to experience if you have healthier skin. Next, list down the tips your dermatologist gave you. You may likewise include tips you found online.

Then, work on a skincare routine. If you already have an effective one, you may simply write it down. In case you want to modify your routine by adding or eliminating a habit, you can create a habit tracker for it.

For your collection on skin care, it also helps to add a calendar for the days you have to exfoliate and the dates you are supposed to meet your dermatologist. If you're trying out a certain skin care product for the first time, you might have to put details about the day you started and the way you're using it.

Every night before you sleep, write down your observations. In case you develop allergic reactions and other undesirable conditions from using the product, discontinue its use and refer to a dermatologist. You can also bring your bujo along to provide more details to your dermatologist about your usage.

PERIOD TRACKER

Female bujo enthusiasts can take advantage of their hobby to help them track their monthly flows. For those who want to get pregnant, they can inform their partners when they're going to be fertile so they can make plans. However, the period tracker shouldn't be used as a birth control method.

CHECKUPS

You should visit your GP and dentist at least once each year. Even if you're living alone, you might want to include your parents' need for such services as well. In case you have your own family, it's even more advisable to include these both in your yearly and in a separate collection in your bujo.

MAJOR OPERATION

Unless you're physically incapable of doing anything, you can make various types of collections based on an upcoming operation or a previous one. For an upcoming operation, you can dedicate a page for counting down the days before the major event in your life. For the post-operation ones, you can make a list about the things you can't do yet, or create a tracker about your progress towards total healing. Make bullet journaling a way of taking care of yourself.

CHAPTER 11:

Business and Financial

Unless it's about an increase in earnings, dealing with your finances can be dull or even stressful. Thankfully, bullet journaling provides a fun way to help you process those expenses, savings, and other finance-related topics.

BUDGET

If you're the type who prefers to do his or her budgeting by writing them down instead of entering items and amounts into a spreadsheet, you might want a collection featuring your fixed and variable expenses in the next month. Before you create your collection though, go over your finances in the last month and the current one. Make a list of recurring finances and those that can vary from time to time.

Your collection on budget doesn't have to be complex. Simply write fixed expenses first and list down their amounts. Then follow it up with the list of variable expenses. Set a certain amount for these things based on last month and this month's expenses. If you're expecting certain events that may affect those, increase or decrease the budget accordingly.

EXPENSE TRACKER

Not everyone feels secured when tracking their expenses using an app. If you're like this, an expense tracker in your bujo will help a lot. This can be placed beside the monthly budget section for easier assessment whether you're sticking to your budget or not.

BOOKKEEPING AND TAX PREPARATION LOGS

Bookkeeping or accounting services can get pretty expensive. One way to reduce the possible cost is by preparing many documents on your own, especially if you're running a business. To help you track the documents you need to prepare, write them down in the future log or in a monthly.

BUSINESS IDEAS

Every now and then, you think about possible solutions to problems which could turn out to be a lucrative business. Don't lose those ideas by keeping them in your bujo. You can dedicate half or an entire page for a business idea. Aside from the business idea, jot down existing problems that it can help resolve. Or, you may also write about an existing problem and list down possible solutions for it.

Bullet journaling may seem complex with the different kinds of collections you can make. However, remembering your past, dictating your present, and planning for your future becomes easier thanks to it.

YOUR 15 DAYS BULLET JOURNAL CHALLENGE

Day 1. / Determine what you want to achieve from bullet journaling.

You may not find bullet journaling that rewarding if you don't even know what kind of rewards you're hoping to get. If you have no clear life goals yet, you can simply focus on what you want to experience for the next 100 days, for this year, or before you hit a certain age. It could encompass your career, family life, health, or investments. It could solely be about your career or relationships. Compile them on a sheet of paper and review it afterwards.

Examples of bullet journaling goals:

- Become more productive at work
- Develop habits to become fitter
- Strengthen bonds
- Handle finances better
- Unleash and improve creative side

Day 2. / List the kinds of collections you'll need to accomplish your goals.

You already know you'll need an index page, as well as one year and several monthly spreads. Decide whether you'll use weekly, daily, or a combination of those two. As for the other types of collections, you can refer to the recommendations in the previous chapters.

If your goals relate to two or more aspects of your life, decide the arrangement of your would-be trackers and other types of collections. As much as possible, monthly trackers should go after your main monthly spread. When it comes to random collections like swatches and entertainment-related ones, they can go after the month-related spreads or be in between weeklies and/or dailies.

Day 3. / Research about possible structures and themes of your pages.

There are plenty of inspirations you can get online. Simply use keywords like bujo, bullet journal, and bullet journaling when searching.

Even if you're aiming for a minimalist bujo, determining the structures beforehand will offer you advantages. It will help your pages look minimalist if the margins and slot sizes of weeklies and dailies are all the same. If you're thinking of drawing boxes for calendars and other bujo entries, you should finalize your decision on this day.

Day 4. / Practice writing, sketching, coloring, painting, and formatting.

For this day, gather scraps of paper and practice writing by hand. Try different pens and other bullet journaling materials as well. To minimize mistakes in your bujo later on, try making drafts of your title pages and initial collections. Create as many drafts as you want and pick your favorite ones later on.

Day 5. / Design your bujo's cover and/or title page.

You decide whether you're going to design your bujo's cover or just leave it as it is. However, it's highly recommended that you create a title page.

For the cover, you can attach pictures or printouts of your name. You can also decorate using washi tapes, stickers, ribbons, and appliques, among others. The options are limitless.

For the title page, you can simply write your name or a title you made up for your bujo. You can even apply calligraphy by featuring a word or a quote you love. It's a great idea to add colors as well. Regardless of the way you decorate the title page, make sure there's an actual title that stands out therein.

Day 6. / Fill your index page/s with your symbols and signifiers.

As a beginner, it will be advisable to stick to the original symbols. However, if you want to be daring and different right from the start, you can decide on your own set of symbols and signifiers. Shapes and colors are among the popular options. You can also use a certain type of washi tape or a stamp, but marking your entries using these could be time-consuming later on.

You should prepare two pages for your index page. It should be right after the title page. You don't have to fill the entire index pages with symbols and signifiers. Leave some space for additional symbols and signifiers. If you think you'll add more later on, reserve the two succeeding pages or the next spread. Don't dedicate just one page as this will make the next challenge a little harder.

Day 7. / Make your future log.

On this day, your bujo starts to become functional. Before you create your future log, get a sheet of paper or open a word processing application to list down events and tasks you have to remember.

If you can't remember the dates, check the reminders in your phone or computer. Ask your loved ones for a list of birthdays and anniversaries as well. Alternatively, you can check their social media profiles for these things.

Don't forget about tasks and events for a certain month, season, or quarter. Check your emails or ask queries regarding subscriptions and upgrades.

Once you're done listing, compile all tasks and events for each month. Instead of experimenting, it's more ideal to stick to a simple future log so you won't likely regret it later on. For your future log, you can reserve the next two or four pages depending on the number of entries.

To make a simple log, attach a calendar or make your own on the left page/s. Arrange the tasks and events, along with their months and dates, on the right page/s.

If you opt for four pages for your future log, the first six months and their corresponding list of events should be on the first spread. The remaining ones should be set on the succeeding spread.

Day 8. / Take a break.

Allow yourself to recharge during this day. The previous challenges may seem simple but it can be stressful if you're a perfectionist. Additionally, you can spend this day trying to gather more inspiration. Moreover, you can use this chance to celebrate your successful first week in bullet journaling.

Day 9. / Work on your monthly page.

Be a step closer to accomplishing your bullet journaling goals by creating your first monthly. For this one, you should contemplate on the current month and what tasks and events you should remember. These tasks can be those finished within this month, those you have yet to start, and those you have yet to accomplish.

When it comes to the events for the month, refer to your future log for birthdays, anniversaries, and other occasions. Then, think of the tasks you're supposed to do for these events. As for events that happened earlier this month, include them in the monthly as well. Those that have yet to happen should be included in a weekly or daily.

To create your first monthly, decide whether it will take a page or two. Once done, draw or attach a small yet visible calendar of the month. It should be on the upper left or upper half of the page or spread. Next, list down the tasks, events, and notes on the remaining space.

Day 10. / Design your dailies.

For your first series of dailies, you can choose to structure them as days pass by or prepare at least four of them at once. A daily can be a quarter, half, or an entire page.

Indicate the date and the day of the week for each daily. The first daily should be about your tasks for tomorrow. You can opt to list down all the tasks first, followed by events. Or, you can write an event first followed by related tasks underneath it. These tasks should include the next challenges for your 15-day bullet journaling journey. Make sure you leave some space for notes.

Day 11. / Starting on this day, mark your days accordingly.

You can refer to your index page about the kind of symbol or signifier you have to use. Mark tasks as completed, incomplete, or incomplete. If you have yet to make your next daily, you can do this during this day.

Day 12. / Sketch, write, or glue pictures of all the things you like.

On this day, you've already covered all four basic collections. It's time to explore another one. Before dwelling on habit trackers and meal plans, show the things you like the most in a page or two.

To do this, get a scrap paper and compile all your favorites therein. These could encompass your hobbies, celebrities, movies, books, places, and thoughts. The collection can be a mixture of words, sketches, or pictures if you want. Once you're done with this page, go back to your daily for this day and mark your tasks accordingly.

Day 13. / Write down your affirmations on a new page.

No matter how lousy your designs are or how few your completed tasks are, you're still doing well. Contemplate on how helpful bullet journaling is so far. Mention those in your next collection which is all about affirmations.

Your affirmations can be specific or broad. Treat it as a way to recognize what you can do and what you have. Don't forget to check your daily and mark your tasks. Prepare your daily for the next day as well, unless you've done this on Day 10.

Day 14. / Create a movie recommendations page.

If you're too focused on your tasks, you might not have time to scour the web for some info about upcoming movie releases. Also, you might have no time watching quality films that are no longer in theaters.

To make up for those, spend your 14th day listing down the movies you want to watch. Don't forget to search for lists of movie releases for this year. You can also look for movie recommendations in your social media circles.

Feature your list of movie recommendations in your bujo. You can arrange them according to the dates of releases or you can group them based on their genres.

If you aren't into movies, you can also go for book or song recommendations. When you're done with your collection, mark your daily for this day and prepare one for tomorrow.

Day 15. / Do a migration.

Starting from the title page to your watchlist or playlist collection, you should already have at least 10 pages filled in your bujo. Furthermore, you already have several tasks that are marked as completed, incomplete, and irrelevant.

By now, you've tried every important step in bullet journaling, except for one: migration. Instead of waiting for the end of the week or month, you can assess what you've accomplished so far when it comes to bullet journaling, and how it has been beneficial to you. Here's your chance to answer whether or not you're closer to accomplishing your bullet journaling goals.

In your initial migration, go over the previous pages and list down vital tasks that you've accomplished. They're basically events now. For the incomplete and unmarked tasks, decide whether they're still relevant. Cross out those you consider irrelevant and include the remaining ones in your list of incomplete tasks featured in your migration page. Then, mark them using the symbol for migrated tasks.

You should also make notes about what kind of tricks work and didn't work for you. On this day, think about what kind of collections you want to do next. Celebrate your completion of the challenges by watching a movie, reading a book, or listening to a song that is one of those recommended in the previous day.

CONCLUSION

I hope this book was able to help you get started with and find joy in bullet journaling. With the guides contained in this book, hopefully you're able to keep a bullet journal that showcases your personality, creativity, and aspirations in life. Most importantly, I wish it will be instrumental in completing your personal and professional goals.

The next step is to commit to bullet journaling on a daily basis or whenever you want. Each session can last for at least a minute of listing down tasks or up to several hours of designing your next monthly, weeklies, and other collections.

I wish you the best of luck!

Printed in Great Britain
by Amazon